nickelodeon

WORMY

Popcorn
ELT
Readers

New Words

What do these new words mean? Ask your teacher or use your dictionary.

caterpillar

Here is a **caterpillar**.

bubble

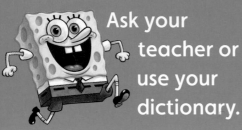

He is making a **bubble**.

crash

The car **crashed** into the bus.

butterfly

The **butterfly** is red and yellow.

destroy

They are **destroying** the house.

jar

This is a **jar**.

look after

They are **looking after** the dog.

monster

The **monster** is horrible.

pet

She has got a lot of **pets**.

save

He **saved** the cat.

'See you soon!'

See you soon!

Verbs

Present	Past
take	took
fly	flew
eat	ate

CHAPTER ONE
A new friend

SpongeBob and Patrick were at Sandy's house.

'I'm going away,' said Sandy. 'Can you look after my pets?'

'Great! I love pets,' said SpongeBob.

SpongeBob and Patrick looked at Sandy's animals.

'You've got a lot of pets,' said Patrick.

'What's in this jar?' asked SpongeBob.

'That's Wormy, my pet caterpillar. He doesn't eat very much,' said Sandy. 'I'm going now. See you soon!'

'What's a caterpillar?' asked Patrick.

'I don't know,' said SpongeBob.

SpongeBob and Patrick looked at Wormy.
'Look at him, Patrick! I love him!'
'Yes, I love him too!'
'Let's play some games,' said SpongeBob.

SpongeBob and Patrick took Wormy out of the jar. They played in the garden. They were very happy.

'It's late now but I don't want to go home,' said Patrick.

'I know,' said SpongeBob. 'Wormy is a great friend.'

'We're going home now, Wormy,' said SpongeBob. He put Wormy in his jar.

Patrick was very sad.

'Don't be sad, Patrick,' said SpongeBob. 'We're going to see Wormy again tomorrow.'

'See you tomorrow, Wormy,' said Patrick.

CHAPTER TWO

Where's Wormy?

The next day SpongeBob and Patrick ran to Sandy's house.

'Let's go and see Wormy,' said SpongeBob.

'Yes, we can play a lot of games again,' said Patrick.

'We're here, Wormy,' said SpongeBob.

But Wormy was not in his jar.

Patrick looked into the jar. There was a big butterfly in it.

'What's that thing?' he asked. 'It's got big eyes and it's horrible.'

'I don't know,' said SpongeBob. 'But it ate Wormy! It's a monster and it's flying out of the jar. Quick, Patrick, run!'

SpongeBob and Patrick were very frightened. They ran to the door.

'Look!' said SpongeBob. 'The monster is in front of the door.'

'We can't go out there,' said Patrick.

They ran away from the butterfly again.

'The monster wants to eat us! It wants to eat all of Sandy's pets!' said SpongeBob. 'But we're going to stop it. Wait for the monster here, Patrick. Then I'm going to jump on it.'

The butterfly flew on to Patrick.

'Please, Mr Monster, don't eat me!' cried Patrick.

'Look at this, Patrick,' said SpongeBob. 'I'm making a bubble.'

The butterfly flew into the bubble.

'We did it!' said SpongeBob. 'We stopped him.'

But the butterfly didn't stop. It flew away in the bubble.

'Oh no!' said SpongeBob. 'It's going to the Krusty Krab. Let's go!'

CHAPTER THREE

A monster at the Krusty Krab

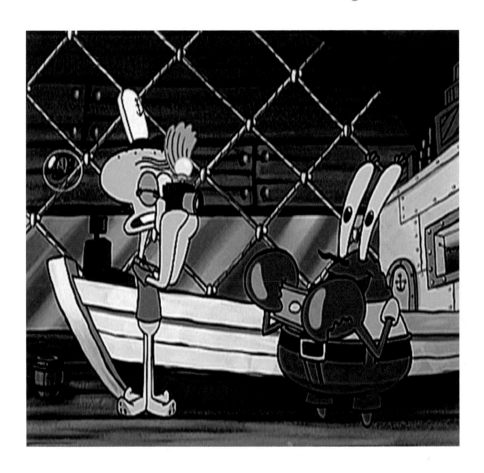

Mr Krabs and Squidward were in the Krusty Krab. Suddenly, SpongeBob and Patrick ran in.

'There's a flying monster in Bikini Bottom!' shouted SpongeBob. 'It's coming here and it's going to eat you!'

'It ate our friend Wormy,' said Patrick.

'Let's all run away!' shouted SpongeBob.

'No, I want to look at this monster,' said Squidward.

'Me too!' said Mr Krabs.

SpongeBob was frightened. He looked into Squidward's eyes. 'Listen to me!' he said. 'The monster is going to eat you!'

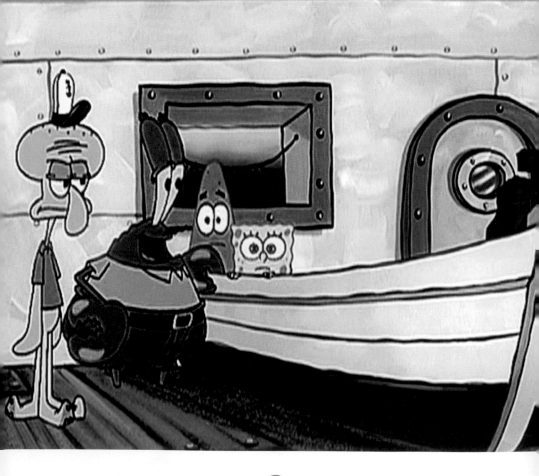

The butterfly came into the Krusty Krab.
SpongeBob and Patrick closed their eyes.

'That's not a monster,' laughed Mr Krabs.

'I like it,' said Squidward.

Then Squidward and Mr Krabs saw the
butterfly's big eyes. Suddenly they were
frightened.

'Argh!' they shouted. They ran away very fast.

SpongeBob opened his eyes again. 'Where are Squidward and Mr Krabs?' he asked. 'The monster ate them! Look, it's flying away. It's going to eat everyone in the town! Let's save them, Patrick.'

'OK,' said Patrick. 'Let's go!'

CHAPTER FOUR
'Run! Everyone run!'

SpongeBob and Patrick ran into the town.

'Listen,' shouted SpongeBob. 'There's a flying monster in Bikini Bottom. It's going to eat you all. Run! Everyone run!'

The butterfly flew into the town.

'Help! It's the flying monster,' everyone shouted.

Everyone was very frightened. They jumped out of their houses and they ran away.

Crash! Bang! They didn't stop and they didn't look. Bang! Ow!

They crashed into things and destroyed them.

'The monster's coming!' they shouted.

'Look, Patrick!' said SpongeBob. 'Everyone is running away. The monster can't eat them now. We saved the town.'

Then they saw the monster again.

'Argh! Run!' they shouted.

A bus stopped in Bikini Bottom. 'I'm home,' said Sandy. 'Oh no! Look at the town! Was it very windy?'

She looked up and down the road. 'Where is everyone?'

Sandy saw her pet.

'Wormy, you're a butterfly now!' she said. 'I'm going to put you back in this jar.'

Everyone in Bikini Bottom ran to Sandy.

'Thank you!' they shouted. 'You stopped the monster and you saved our town.'

THE END

CORAL REEFS

SpongeBob lives in Bikini Bottom. Bikini Bottom is a coral reef. Let's read more about coral reefs.

WHAT IS CORAL?

Polyps are very small animals but they do not move. Millions of polyps make a coral. Millions of corals make a reef. Corals can be many shapes and colours. They are very beautiful. They like the light from the sun.

polyps

coral

SAVE THE REEFS

Coral reefs are home to a lot of animals. There are coral reefs in only 1% of the sea but 25% of sea animals and fish live in them!

Pollution destroys coral reefs very quickly. Today people want to stop pollution and save the reefs.

saving the reefs

Did you know...?

The Great Barrier Reef in Australia is 20,000 years old and 2,000 km long. That is a lot of polyps!

★
What else can you find under the sea?
★

What do these words mean? Find out.

millions   shape
colour   fish   pollution

After you read

1 True (✓) or False (✗)? Write in the box.

a) Sandy went away. ✓

b) Wormy was SpongeBob's pet. ☐

c) Patrick was frightened of the monster. ☐

d) The monster destroyed Bikini Bottom. ☐

e) SpongeBob saved Bikini Bottom. ☐

f) The flying monster was Sandy's pet, Wormy. ☐

2 Circle the correct word.

a) SpongeBob and Patrick played *garden* / *games* with Wormy.

b) Wormy lived in *a house* / *a jar*.

c) SpongeBob made *a bubble* / *a butterfly*.

d) The butterfly *ran* / *flew* to the Krusty Krab.

e) Squidward and Mr Krabs *liked* / *ate* the monster.

f) In Bikini Bottom they *jumped into* / *jumped out of* their houses.

Where's the popcorn?
Look in your book.
Can you find it?

Puzzle time!

1 Make one word from the green letters and one word from the red letters.

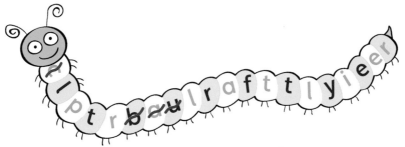

a) <u>c</u> <u>a</u> _ _ _ _ _ _ _ _ _   b) <u>b</u> <u>u</u> _ _ _ _ _ _

2 Where did the butterfly go? Write four more sentences. Use the words in the box.

into   onto   ~~into~~   behind   under

a) The butterfly flew into the garden.
b) ....
c) ....
d) ....
e) ....

3 Find the butterflies and caterpillars and write the numbers.

a) __Three__ butterflies are drinking.

b) _____ butterflies are flying.

c) _____ caterpillars are eating .

d) _____ caterpillars are walking.

e) _____ caterpillars are sleeping.

4 What's your favourite pet? Tick and then ask some friends.

Animal		You	Friends		
Dog					
Cat					
Bird					
Fish					
Rabbit					

Imagine...

Imagine you have a pet. What is it? What is its English name? Talk to a friend.

I've got a fish. Its name is Fishy.

I've got a bird. Its name is Coral.

Chant

1 🎧 Listen and read.

Let's play!

Let's play games with Wormy!
Wormy is our friend.
We can run and play all day
And tomorrow play again.

There's a monster in Wormy's jar,
Oh no! It's coming out!
It's going to eat everyone,
Let's run away and shout …
Aaaaaaaaaaaaaarrrr!

2 🎧 Say the chant.